PROJECT LEARNING USING DIGITAL PORTFOLIOS

HOW TO CREATE DIGITAL PORTFOLIOS FOR PROBLEM SOLVING AND INNOVATION

IV THURSTON

Rosen
YA

New York

Published in 2018 by The Rosen Publishing Group, Inc.
29 East 21st Street, New York, NY 10010

Library of Congress Cataloging-in-Publication Data

Names: Thurston, IV, author.
Title: How to create digital portfolios for problem solving and innovation / IV Thurston.
Description: First edition. | New York, New York : Rosen Publishing, 2018. | Series: Project learning using digital portfolios | Includes bibliographical references and index. | Audience: 7-12.
Identifiers: LCCN 2016059454 | ISBN 9781508175261 (library bound)
Subjects: LCSH: File organization (Computer science)—Juvenile literature. | Digital media—Juvenile literature. | Inventions—Marketing—Juvenile literature. | Employment portfolios—Juvenile literature.
Classification: LCC QA76.9.F5 H69 2018 | DDC 005.74/1--dc23
LC record available at https://lccn.loc.gov/2016059454

Manufactured in China

CONTENTS

You've been a student for what seems like years, and you have learned so much. You have things you are proud of, things you think might be good and useful to show somebody someday, but how do you do it? Do you just hand someone a stack of papers or a couple of photographs, or play them a video on your smartphone? How would that even work? What if the person you want to show off your work to does not even live near you? What then? You are in luck because now you can make a digital portfolio.

Digital portfolios are here to stay. They can be as simple or as elaborate as you like. There was a time when you couldn't have things like video in your portfolio because portfolios were just paper. Now, however, with the ability to load files on the web, or on your desktop embedded in a PDF, you have more options and more flexibility than ever before. Besides, each day, more and more colleges and universities are requiring digital portfolios as part of the admissions process. Additionally, digital portfolios can be shared. There is a real advantage to having teachers or parents or even your friends being able to share their thoughts with you as you develop your digital portfolio.

You can also use your digital portfolio as a platform to work with a teacher to problem solve something. For example, you are writing a report on Native Americans and you have a draft of your report but you aren't fully confident about it. Share it with a teacher and she can offer comments that might help you out. Not all problems are so obvious,

Technology allows for more options than ever before when creating your digital portfolio. Digital portfolios let you share your work with people no matter where they are.

though, and so there are tons of problem-solving strategies and techniques within this book to help you succeed in today's ever-changing landscape. Reading about the best American artists of all time, a few great thinkers, problem solving, and innovation can give you some ideas to stand out from the crowd.

CHAPTER ONE

TODAY IS THE DAY TO CREATE A DIGITAL PORTFOLIO

T oday is the big day. You're going to apply to an intense science program. You're smart. You've done all the work, but so have all of the other students applying. You have taken tests, and so have they. You have great recommendation letters from your teachers; they have letters from their teachers. How can you separate yourself from the pack? Until recently, there weren't too many options, but now, with the rise of cloud computing and other technological breakthroughs, there is: a digital portfolio.

A portfolio provides a record of things you have done that you can show other people. It is a more inclusive record than a report card. A report card is a record that cannot be updated: you took a series of tests and had homework, papers, and all the rest, and now it is done. A portfolio, on the other hand, is a document storage system that you can change when there are new things to add or when you want to present a particular side of yourself. In that way, a portfolio

Portfolios used to be a collection of documents that you would have to hand deliver to people. Since you don't have to carry them, digital portfolios give you the option to have more than one.

is a tool that you can use to shape how people see you. When you select what goes into your portfolio you let people see you and get an idea of who you are before they meet you. In fact, portfolios can show other people what you know and how you use it. They can even learn about what strategies you use to solve problems. But don't think you can only have one portfolio. As long as they are neat and focused, you can have more than one—after all, you're a well-rounded person. For example, if you are interested in both science and art, two different portfolios would make perfect sense. Your science portfolio would showcase all of the lab work you have done. It could also show tests, papers, or even documentation from the science fair you attended. Your fine-art portfolio, on the other hand, could be full of drawings and photographs of paintings and sculptures, even your best Instagram pictures, as well as any awards you may have won. All the work in both portfolios is yours, but you are focusing on one aspect when introducing yourself to others.

Speaking of art, portfolios were traditionally what artists of all sorts (graphic designers, fine artists, interior designers, and photographers) used to find jobs. If you made images for a living, a traditional résumé wouldn't work. You needed to have a physical record of what you created. For years it was common to see advertising professionals running up and down Madison Avenue in New York City carrying what looked like large black folders into interviews to show samples of their work. Some examples were corporate logos, advertisements, or even photographs. These days, however, you don't have to be a graphic designer to have a portfolio. More and more people are building portfolios. In fact, portfolios are not just for professionals anymore. More and more students are building portfolios while they are in school. These serve as artifacts

TIME CAPSULES AND PORTFOLIOS

Perhaps you are wondering what the difference is between a time capsule and a digital portfolio. With a portfolio, you arrange things to tell a story—be it about what you've learned or something you are building toward. A time capsule, on the other hand, is completely frozen in time. Another way to look at it is that a time capsule is meant to preserve things: newspapers, artifacts, and memories. A portfolio is a living document. Another difference is that time capsules are usually buried in the ground or put in a building's cornerstone as a celebration of a special occasion. They're not opened or even touched until a specific set date. Your portfolio is designed for personal use.

Digital portfolios offer many advantages over traditional paper portfolios. They are easier to organize and arrange when new material is added. With traditional paper portfolios, a person would have to reshuffle all of the papers in the binder and make sure they were handled with care so they stay neat looking. A digital portfolio makes it less complicated since you can drag and drop images or text, and then the software takes care of the rest. Also, consider the example mentioned earlier: walking all around New York City with a paper portfolio is tiring and time consuming. Appointments have to be made, the portfolio has to be carried no matter what the

(continued on the next page)

(continued from the previous page)

What's the difference between a portfolio and a time capsule? Portfolios can be changed whenever you like, a time capsule is meant as a specific record.

weather—all these headaches! All of this is avoided with a digital portfolio. Today you can email people a link, send people a USB, or burn a CD. The options are endless and growing with each passing day!

of work you have done. In addition to the fact that portfolios are no longer the exclusive purview of artists, with the rapid adaptation of digital technology in both the educational world and professional workplace, these days many portfolios are completely digital.

In an article for the *Buffalo News,* Jack Weibel, a recently retired Graphics staffer for over forty-five years, remembers working back in the analog days. In those days, there was a lot of handiwork. You were constantly cutting and pasting text and images. Today, through the rise of Adobe as the premier design suite used by publishers, there is more creative freedom for design. Weibel also discusses the changes he saw over the years in both how things were made at the newspaper and how applicants' portfolios changed: "I had worked for two advertising agencies prior to my job at the news. When the job came up I went through some of the printed works that I thought were portfolio ready and then I stayed up all night mounting them."

Now you may think of riding a horse when you read the word "mount," but there was a time when people building their portfolios would meticulously cut out various works they thought represented themselves the best and then mount them onto poster board or foam to show their work. After mounting everything, Weibel then put them in the ubiquitous black

portfolio presenter and would go to his interview. How fortu-
nate we are now to be able to easily change things digitally!

Besides moving from India ink and rulers to create maps to
using Adobe Illustrator and Photoshop, Weibel also touched
upon how the presentation of portfolios changed over the
years: "By the mid-1990's everything had gone digital with

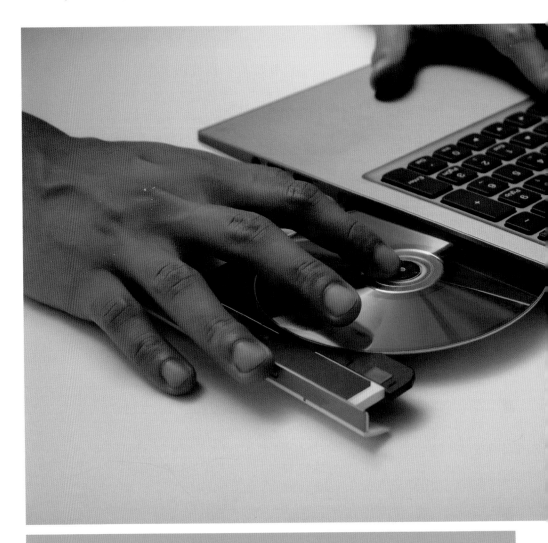

Graphic designer Jack Weibel remembers that "By the mid-1990's
everything had gone digital . . . In terms of portfolios, people would
give us a CD-ROM."

very few exceptions. In terms of portfolios, people would give us a CD-ROM or something like that, but it wasn't until iPads and other tablets became common, that portfolios started getting more dynamic. Now instead of handing over your portfolio, if everyone has a device, people can flip through them like a book."

DIGITAL PORTFOLIOS FOR STUDENTS

The last few years have seen a steady increase in the use of digital portfolios by students. In fact, some schools, like Grandview High School in Washington State, have put them at the heart of their curriculum. Portfolios for students can work in any number of ways. On the most basic level, it is a storage system of past accomplishments. However, a dynamic digital portfolio with inputs and outputs can be an active space allowing for collaboration, problem solving, and a chance to reflect. By thinking about what to include in your portfolio, and the order you select, you develop a deeper knowledge and understanding of the work in your portfolio. This type of reflection makes you a better student as you are actively paying attention to your education. It can also help identify strengths and weaknesses that otherwise could go unnoticed. You may find, for example, that history is a weakness for you. By curating your portfolio you can learn new things about yourself. This allows you to adjust your focus and come up with a plan of action. Many educators believe that portfolios not only show what students have accomplished but can also act as a roadmap to where they are going. Students can explore future careers that they may be interested in and keep track of academic achievements.

There has never been an easier time to create a digital portfolio. Computers are in schools in unprecedented numbers, with the most recent statistics saying that there is a computer for every five students in US public schools. There have been massive efforts made to bring high-speed Internet to even the most remote school districts in the land. Recently, more standardized tests were taken digitally than on paper for the first time ever,

Once only in computer labs, now it is common for every classroom throughout America to have a computer in it.

and there is no sign of going back. In Canada, very similar things are occurring. The student-to-computer ratio is competitive with the United States, and 97 percent of teachers have at least one computer in the classroom, with 93 percent having access to the Internet. Teachers have commented that digital technologies, and therefore digital portfolios, allow students to share their work with a wider audience, increase collaboration with other students and fuel innovation, and increase students self-directing their education. As access to technology continues to grow, more and more schools will require students to keep a digital portfolio. The time to create one is now.

CHAPTER TWO

WHAT TO INCLUDE AND HOW TO ORGANIZE YOUR DIGITAL PORTFOLIO

As you know, online portfolios are a great tool to show off your skills, talents, and projects to your teachers and fellow classmates, as well as friends and family. The first step, of course, is building one. Like anything else, the first time you build your portfolio will be the most time consuming, but it will be worth it! Putting serious time and effort into how you construct your portfolio will help it stand out from the rest of the pack. Show people that you know how to properly value your work and that you take yourself seriously by building a portfolio that shines!

In order to create a successful portfolio, you should

Setting up your first portfolio will take time, but it is worth it! The next one will be done in half the time.

have one or two objectives for your portfolio and make sure you never waver from them. There are many elements that go into a great digital portfolio. Here are a few key things to make sure to include:

- **Background Information.** Here is your chance to show your personality! Some people skip this step even though it is one of the most important. What makes you unique? Are you the class clown always brightening people's day? Show that off. Include a picture of yourself that you want to use to represent yourself to the world. Keep in mind, though, that silly photos are great with friends, but not for your portfolio. Also include where you are from. What is your town or city like? Do you take the subway to school, or is your grade made up of only twenty people? These are the little details that will help set you apart.
- **Course Work.** What are some of the major projects that you want to include? You should make one the cornerstone of your portfolio. Perhaps you worked closely on a team project? That would be something great to include to show off how well you work with others.
- **Awards.** Did you win an award in a competition? Did you work with other students or by yourself to win your school's science fair? That would be a perfect cornerstone of a portfolio.
- **Community Service.** Do you do volunteer work through your school, civic organization, or religious organization? Not everyone does those things, and that is what makes you special. Show it off in your portfolio!
- **Testimonials.** Perhaps you have a teacher that you have worked very closely with. If you do have such a person in your academic life, consider having him or her write a

testimonial on your behalf. This will also be good practice before you apply to colleges, as you will need letters of recommendation from teachers.

- **List of Skills.** Do you have any skills that are not common for everyone else in your grade? Are you the young hacker? Let the world know that you can code and use CSS! Can you speak Mandarin Chinese? That is something that will set you apart, so let everyone know and include it in your digital portfolio!
- **Media Mentions.** Maybe your sports team won a championship and your picture was in the paper. Include it! Or, when you won your school's invention convention and were mentioned in an article. Include it!

A portfolio is your chance to make yourself stand out. What makes you special? Make sure to include things like awards won.

Since your portfolio is going to be digital, keep in mind that pictures are great and videos are even better. Facebook, for example, has found that people are much more likely to click on news stories and advertisements that have images. People want your portfolio to be easy to navigate and engaging. Photography and video help ensure that your portfolio is dynamic. This is something to keep in mind as you continue to create potential content for your portfolio. If you enter your school's science fair, take as many pictures as possible. Do you have a solo coming up for a school concert? This would be a perfect time to have video to supplement your portfolio.

ORGANIZING YOUR FILES

Now that you know what to include in your digital portfolio, it is now time to organize all of your work to make building your digital portfolio as easy as possible. Maybe up until now you have never given much thought to organization, and that is OK, but if you stick to a system and use it from this day forward, updating your digital portfolio will be very easy. If you aren't quite sure whether or not your computer is poorly organized, see how many of these apply to you:

- Your desktop is cluttered with more than thirty different things
- "My Documents" is your catchall for documents, photos, audio files, and more
- The way you find files is by searching for them
- A single file is in more than one folder

If you recognize yourself in any of these, it is time to organize. Still not convinced? Perhaps you are thinking, "I have always just

While it isn't exactly the most fun thing to do, organizing your files now will make creating your digital portfolio—and doing anything else on your computer—much easier later.

searched for files, I can keep doing it!" And for a while you might be fine, but if you find yourself looking for a group of similar files—like all of the files that you want to put in your digital portfolio—it will be difficult. There are different ways of finding a file. You would want to have the best arrangement for yourself. You can find it by name, by type, and, if it's a photograph, by image. If you're working on a project with others, you will have to make sure they can find the files as well. Once you start collaborating with other people, having an organizational system for your files is a must!

Before we begin thinking about how to organize, a disclaimer is in order: there is no one best approach to organizing your files. There are, however, a series of practices that you can use as a guide as you customize your system. One of the best ways to name your files is to start with the most general information and work your way to the most specific. A great way to start is with the date. The most common way to arrange dates is by year, month, and date (often abbreviated as YYYYMMDD). For example, if you start a report for history class on the Constitutional Convention on April 18, 2018, the file name would start with 20180418. The next thing to put in the file name is an underscore (_). While some computer operating systems support leaving a blank space in a file name, others do not, so it is best to avoid that potential problem. Also, the underscore is universal for file names, so others will already know what you mean. Avoid using special characters such as !, #, *, &, or ^ , especially if these file names will end up on the Internet, where they can cause lots of unintended problems. Next, you should have your name in the file. Here there are a few options. You can have your first initial followed by your family name, or your family name first followed by your name. If you use your first initial followed by your family name, remember to capitalize your family name. In the example we are using, let's say the report is being written by Rebecca Jefferson. The file name would then look like this 20180418_RJefferson. Finally, add the actual name of the file. In our example, "Constitutional Convention." Assuming this is written in Microsoft Word, the final name of our file would be 20180418_RJefferson_Constitutional Congress.doc.

Once the file name has been determined, it is time to figure out how to organize all the files you will be using to create your digital portfolio. Using everything we've talked about earlier, Rebecca might organize the content of her digital portfolio by starting off with a folder called "current projects." Nestled in that folder there would be a folder called "20170418_RJefferson_digital portfolio." Within that folder would be folders for all of the elements discussed earlier: background information, course work (which is where the file 20180418_RJefferson_ConstitutionalCongress.doc would be), awards, community service, testimonials, list of skills, and media mentions. To focus on course work, the setup could look like this:

We all have multiple devices: computers, phones, tablets. And they are interacting now more than ever. Creating a system and sticking to it will make all the interactions much easier.

20170418_RJefferson_digital portfolio > course work > history > 20180418_RJefferson_ConstitutionalCongress.doc, and then you would simply create a new folder for each subject.

DO I EVEN NEED A DIGITAL PORTFOLIO?

With the rise of the Common Application for colleges and universities, there has never been a greater commitment to the digital world than there is right now. Years ago, when the Common Application began, numerous public and private places of higher learning met to discuss what they felt high schools, and their students, should be focusing on. One of the initiatives that came out of that meeting was creating a new online platform for digital portfolios. The hope was to get ninth graders to reflect on what they are learning in high school. They also wanted students to receive feedback from admissions departments. These were ways to help level the playing field between those who live in school districts that are well funded and have a greater number of support staff like guidance counselors and those who don't.

The basic idea works like this: all students will have the opportunity to have a free, online digital portfolio and begin adding to it when they enter high school. Students can control their privacy settings, and college admissions leaders can ask questions and help students refine their digital portfolios throughout their high school careers, giving them an extra advantage when it is finally time to apply for college or university. Hopefully the idea of "padding" an application with numerous activities that a student truly isn't passionate about in order to look better will give way and be replaced by a more significant experience that reflects what motivates a student.

Not everyone has immediately embraced these ideas. Some have pointed out that not everyone has equal access to computers, so things can never be truly fair. Others offer the criticism that a universal application system might just further the homogenization of education culture. No matter what problems people may have, it is clear that this system is not going to go away anytime soon.

WHERE SHOULD YOU HOST YOUR PORTFOLIO?

Fortunately, the web is now teeming with places to host your digital portfolio, and many of them are free. The following places have a proven track record of being great places to host your digital portfolio.

- **Yola.com.** This website promises to allow you to create your portfolio in only thirty minutes. The site features drag-and-drop site building to make your digital portfolio creation painless. It is ad free and also allows you to have complete control over your portfolio if you are familiar with basic web coding.
- **Jimdo.com.** Jimdo works in a way that is similar to Tumblr. This site provides users with numerous templates to choose and work from. An advantage of Jimdo is that it is designed to

be mobile responsive, so your digital portfolio will look good on a mobile device, too. Its best feature is that you can also easily edit your portfolio from your phone.

- **Weebly.com.** Like Jimdo, Weebly has numerous templates to choose from and offers the advantage of having a specific portfolio grouping of templates to work with. Weebly also has drag-and-drop site building and mobile editing that syncs across all devices, so when you edit something on your phone, the changes will immediately show up on a tablet or computer. This gives you more freedom to change information whenever you need to.

- **Silkapp.com.** Silk offers the option of sharing collections of materials or writing on a web page like a blog. Silk's dashboard allows you to easily organize all of the various aspects of your digital portfolio, including documents, videos, images, graphs, and links to other sites. Another great thing about Silk is that your site can be collaborative, allowing you to have other people be editors on your website.

- **Dsitesropr.com.** Dropr allows you to create digital portfolios with videos, images, and even audio files. You can also have multiple portfolios all with different URLs. Dropr requires only an email address or a social media profile to get started, and like some of the sites above, allows free drag-and-drop portfolio building from your desktop. Dropr also allows your digital portfolio to be embedded in other websites (like your personal blog) as a slideshow.

- **eduClipper.net.** eduClipper is a unique digital portfolio–building tool. If you happen to already be using eduClipper at your school, then this is your best bet. It allows you to use the things you have already "clipped" (bookmarked) online, it works well with Google Drive, and it lets you use your work from other places where you may have generated content online. The interface is the same between eduClipper for portfolios and eduClipper for bookmarking to make things easier.

- **sites.google.com.** Google Sites is an extremely powerful tool. It allows you to make your digital portfolio as complex as you wish it to be. Like the other digital portfolio hosts mentioned, it attempts to make creating your digital portfolio as easy as editing a document. You can add text, videos, presentations, files, and more to build your customized digital portfolio. Like Silk, Google Sites also allows you to bring in people to collaborate on your digital portfolio as long as you already have a Google Drive. Also, with the more advanced settings, you can allow someone to collaborate on only a single part of your digital portfolio instead of allowing the person access to your entire website.

There are numerous places to host your digital portfolio and internet giant Google is one spot to do it. As long as your partner has Google Drive, you can collaborate on a portfolio together.

- **PortfolioGen.com.** The advantage of PortfolioGen is that it was designed specifically for students and teachers to build dynamic digital portfolios. In addition to the features listed in the other digital portfolio hosts listed above, PortfolioGen allows you to ask for endorsements from teachers and other students. It also features a guest book that allows visitors to leave comments on your digital portfolio.

Students and teachers have previously tested these sites above, so what are you waiting for? As you get older, you become busier with life. Now is the time to start your digital portfolio.

CHAPTER THREE

DIFFERENT WAYS TO SOLVE A PROBLEM

No matter what you are doing, no matter what you are working on, eventually you will run into a mental roadblock. This is completely normal, and it happens all the time. The question is, how are you going to handle it? Your best option is to construct a creative problem-solving tool kit with different strategies that can be used whenever you are stuck and are unsure what to do next. Additionally, having a group of techniques to help solve problems makes you a more valuable member of the community. Perhaps at one point memorizing and repeating were the best techniques to

Eventually you will run into a mental roadblock. The key is to be ready with strategies to help you solve your problem.

learn, but as things are changing rapidly, having the ability to creatively adapt will help set you apart as the star you are.

CREATIVE PROBLEM SOLVING

Creative problem solving focuses on the exciting possibilities of creative and critical thinking. It can also help you learn how to be better prepared for life and all of its many changes and challenges. The best part is, no matter what you want to do with your life, these tools will always be useful.

One of the best things you can do when you run into a problem is to rephrase the problem. Sometimes it is easy to get caught up in how something is said and the language becomes a distraction from the actual goal of solving your problem. For example, a teacher asked you to write about "how the Louisiana Purchase changed America" and you are having a very hard time thinking about anything besides the fact that the Louisiana Purchase made America larger. Perhaps the best thing to do in this situation is to rephrase the problem and think about "how the Louisiana Purchase made America stronger." Notice how you are still answering the original question, but that simple change in words changed your entire point of view. Play with the sentence and use different words to see if it can help unlock your brain. Instead of using the word "changed," perhaps "improved" or "benefitted" could lead to a breakthrough!

Another strategy that is often used in solving problems is known as chunking. Every problem is a piece of a larger problem. Maybe when you were younger you used to ask your parents questions all the time—maybe it even drove them crazy! Bring back the questions as a way to break up larger things into smaller parts. An example of chunking could be applied to making a digital portfolio. Ask yourself, "Why do I

You are about to enter a time of your life that will present many new challenges. Being prepared will help you rise to the occasion and shine!

want to make a digital portfolio?" "To go to a good university," you might say. Then the next question is, "Why do I want to go to a good university?" and the answer to that might be, "Because I want to work in government." Now the question to ask switches from "why" to "what": "What should I put in my digital portfolio to show a university that I want to go there so I can work in government some day?" By asking basic question you are able to break down the larger problem of creating a digital portfolio into something much more basic and something that does a much better job of reflecting your own goals. Also, notice how in this example with each question asked you were better able to define for yourself what

ALBERT EINSTEIN: THE GREATEST PROBLEM SOLVER OF ALL TIME?

Chances are you have heard of Albert Einstein. With his unkempt hair and mustache, he is instantly recognizable. He is arguably the most famous physicist ever, and he is one of history's greatest problem solvers. Einstein has been quoted as saying, "If I had an hour to solve a problem, I'd spend 55 minutes thinking about the problem and five minutes thinking about the solution." What do you think that means? One way to approach this quotation is to realize that Einstein himself would approve of the numerous problem-solving strategies that have been outlined. Einstein was famous for not always following the lead of his peers and approaching problems with unique strategies.

Scientists were trying to figure out what space was made of. They decided that space was made of something they called ether and that everything moves through it. However, the more experiments they did, the farther away they were getting from proving that ether existed. In 1905, Einstein published a paper that approached the problem from a new perspective. He wrote that since we don't know if we are moving through ether or not, it is better not to think of ether at all since it was distracting from the real problem. This created many new ideas, in particular, that there is no such thing as one kind of time. Einstein's amazing problem-solving skills proved that time is not the same for everyone. Experiments were done with two

"It's not that I'm so smart, it's just that I stay with problems longer." If Albert Einstein could find the time to slowly come up with a solution, you can, too!

(continued on the next page)

(continued from the previous page)

identical clocks, one on an airplane traveling east and one still on the ground. What was found was that the clock on the plane, moving in addition to Earth's rotation, was slightly slower.

Here is another quote from Einstein that shows just how important creative problem solving is: "We cannot solve our problems with the same thinking we used when we created the problem." Like so much of what Einstein said, this is not as simple as it sounds. How can we invent a new way of seeing the world and changing our outlook to help us solve problems, problems that are often of our own making? Well, don't worry. Einstein uses his own experience to offer this piece of advice: "It's not that I'm so smart, it's just that I stay with problems longer." So don't quit! No matter how hard the problem is, or how impossible it seems to fix, Albert Einstein believes in you!

you wanted to do, and just by defining your goal you were better able to solve the problem.

Empathy is an extremely valuable character trait to have. This next technique can help you develop it. Before acting too quickly, try and look at a problem from different perspectives. A simple change in your point of view can instantly open up whatever difficulty you might be facing, providing fresh new angles. In the example above, think about the answer to the question "Why do I want a digital portfolio?" from the point of view one of your teachers. Your parents. Your best friend. A college admissions professional. Look at it from each of these angles. This could quite easily unlock a new strategy that you didn't even know you were missing!

You might have noticed that many of these problem-solving strategies involve changing the language that the problem is presented in. There is a reason for that. How we say things influences what we think about them. For example, try to make things positive. Things that are phrased in the negative take longer for our brains to process and can distract from finding a successful solution to a problem. Instead of thinking, "How can I not play video games as much?" you would be much better off asking yourself, "How can I improve my grades?"

Phrasing things in the positive is much more motivating, and oftentimes the real goal is hidden behind the negative language. Another phrasing option is to begin your question with, "In what ways might I…" You'll find that just by using a word like "ways," your brain automatically starts looking for multiple solutions instead of one. Additionally, sometimes you might think that the problem you are facing is just a bit dull or completely boring. When that is the case, it is up to you to make the problem a bit more exciting. Instead of asking yourself why you would want to create a digital portfolio, you should ask how you can make a digital portfolio that would amaze your friends. Your brain will thank you for it! By using these techniques, you will come up with a list of behaviors that you know to avoid in order to have a better report card!

Finally, a technique that works very well and that focuses less on language is called mind mapping. All you'll need is a piece of paper, a picture or image that represents your problem, and things to write with. Place the picture or image in the middle of your paper and from there draw different branches and write down your ideas. Your brain is hard-wired to organize things, and you will start seeing connections between different ideas that you didn't know existed until you started writing them down.

WHAT ABOUT BRAINSTORMING?

Chances are pretty high that you have been in a brainstorming session. Especially in a classroom setting, brainstorming is the easiest approach to take to solve a problem and generate ideas. The rules are simple: any idea is fine during the brainstorming session and there are no judgements. However, brainstorming isn't as effective as allowing people to work by themselves. There are a few problems with brainstorming, especially in a classroom, that are too often ignored:

- **Only One Person Can Talk at a Time.** Of course, this makes sense. Whoever is writing things down can't hear multiple people, and in the

While extremely common, brainstorming is not always the best approach for problem solving. If you are leading a brainstorming session, make sure you ask the quieter people for their ideas.

time you need to wait to tell everyone your idea, you can't think about new ones!

- **People Get Nervous.** Even if the idea is to create a place free of judgments, there will still be people privately judging others' ideas. Also, even if all of your classmates were to suspend judgment, there is still a strong possibility that a student will be nervous to offer his or her opinion.

- **Personality Problems.** We are all different people, with different learning styles! Those who crave attention will speak the most, quieter people will shy away from saying anything, and people who get jealous easily might not accept other ideas that they did not come up with.

Instead of brainstorming, there is a new idea called brainwriting. Everyone is still gathered together to try and solve a problem. However, instead of talking at the same time, everyone is given a few minutes to write down as many ideas as possible to help solve a problem. After a few minutes have passed, everyone passes their paper to the person next to them and the cycle repeats itself. Once there have been enough ideas or it is becoming very difficult to come up with new ideas, papers are collected and then the better ideas are

Brainwriting is a newer idea that is gaining in popularity. Everyone in a group is given a few minutes to generate ideas, then they are collectively shared and discussed.

gathered and discussed just like in regular brainstorming. The benefits are immediate:

- **More Ideas.** When you don't have to wait to add your idea to the list, you create more ideas. Also, since sheets are shared, other people still get exposed to new ideas before they begin to create more of their own.
- **Everyone Participates.** Because you have to share your ideas with other people, no one can hide and let the people who enjoy speaking in public do all the work. Also, everyone has an equal voice. No one can "write louder" and prevent others from being heard.

Although there are some negatives when it comes to brainstorming and brainwriting, they are both still great for you to do before you start on your digital portfolio. When you brainstorm, you create ideas. Your ideas are what your portfolio could potentially look like. Your portfolio could include photos, text, and audio, as well as video. By brainstorming, you give yourself time to make your portfolio the best that it can be.

Brainwriting is great for those who are a bit less creative. If you have friends or peers that are better at the creative aspect of portfolios, let them give you some pointers on colors and images. You may have the text, but the design could be the reason why a future school or employer welcomes you.

CHAPTER FOUR

INNOVATION!

There are numerous tools that you could use to solve problems, but there is an innovative new tool to add to your toolbox, and it is called design thinking. Many of the most innovative companies in the world, companies such as Apple, Coca-Cola, Nike, and Proctor & Gamble, use this practice.

WHAT IS DESIGN THINKING?

Everything you currently own that was made by someone else had to have been originally designed. Everything. Designers are some of our most creative and innovative problem solvers. They are concerned with what could be, as opposed to what is. Learning to think this way can help anyone, no matter if they are a student or a surgeon. Design thinking does not focus on problems. The idea is to focus on solutions for a future that you would like to see. Combining logic with imagination can create new outcomes.

NECESSITY IS THE MOTHER OF INVENTION

The phrase "Necessity is the mother of invention" is often attributed to the ancient Greek philosopher Plato in his book *Republic*, but the phrase was already being used in English prior to translations of the book, so it was more likely added by a translator as opposed to being written by Plato himself.

Have you ever thought about what this phrase might mean? It pretty much means that we, as a people, have figured out how to create things that never existed before because we had no choice. This goes for anything. A great example was the invention of the wheel. It is incredible to think that there was a time before the wheel, as it seems so obvious today. However, thousands of years ago the only way to get something like wheat from the field to where you lived was to carry it, drag it, or push it. Then one day, perhaps, there was a farmer who had a crop of wheat that was greater than normal that day and who didn't want to make multiple trips to and from the pile. He must have seen a log on the ground and got the ingenious idea to use it to help roll the wheat back to the house.

Not all inventions have to be as groundbreaking as the invention of the wheel! Perhaps you can think of some more nefarious examples? Here is one to get you started: you have probably seen in cartoons or in a movie a prisoner being held in a tower or high off of the ground. The prisoner may have tied bedsheets together to make a rope to rappel down the side of the building to be able to escape. Necessity is the mother of invention, indeed! What are some fun examples of necessity being the mother of invention that you can think of?

Plato is perhaps wrongly credited with the phrase "Necessity is the mother of invention." Sometimes we don't know who was the first to say something or invent something, but we still get to benefit!

Design thinking is a simple five-step process:

- **Empathize.** Empathy, even in an innovative method like design thinking, is still important. The idea is to work to really understand something from the point of view of the person you are making your digital portfolio for. Using previous examples that you've learned, what would someone in a university admissions office want to see in a portfolio of a potential student who wants to work in government someday? This requires some imagination and some research! All admissions officials would like to see good grades and extracurricular activities, but what is unique to students at their school?

- **Define.** Once you have gathered information from step one, decide who your admissions official is: how old is the person? What does he or she like? Make your digital portfolio with that person you have invented as your audience.

- **Ideate.** Along with step one, this is the step that allows for the most creativity. This is the verb form of "idea." There are no ideas that are too wild in this stage. The more ideas you have, the better!

- **Prototype.** This is the stage where you edit some of your ideas and begin to actually make a digital portfolio (or several). Make sure that you interact with it to see if you think it accomplished what you set out to do in the first place.

- **Test.** There are no grades here, but this is when you would allow others to explore your digital portfolio. You want to learn what they think of it. Was it easy to use? Was there something they wished was there that isn't? If they were a university admissions official, would this make them want to bring you to the campus? If so, why? If not, why not?

A CRISIS IN ART:
INNOVATION AND PAINTING

We often think of innovations in technology as applying to the sciences, but the effects of innovation are felt in all fields. For example, after the invention and widespread use of photography to capture lifelike images, fine art painters found themselves with a new challenge: If photography can capture images better than a paintbrush, what is the point of painting? As you know, necessity is the mother of all invention, and never was this statement more true!

Most experts agree that, starting with the Impressionists, artists began to think of ways that paint could capture the world in a way that a photograph cannot. With their use of color and brush strokes to capture the feeling of a place, Impressionists set the table for abstraction in the visual arts. Painting continued to move even farther away from realistic depictions with styles like Cubism. Pablo Picasso, perhaps the most famous visual artist of the twentieth century, would paint the same object from multiple angles, breaking it down into simple shapes. After World War II, New York City saw the rise of Abstract Expressionism (the splatter painters) with artists such as Jackson Pollock not even attempting to reflect anything of the physical world and making painting more about brushwork and composition (the balance of color and shapes on the canvas).

(continued on the next page)

(continued from the previous page)

Jackson Pollock was an innovator in American painting. Since he wanted to drip painting onto the canvas, his first innovation was to put it on the floor!

By the 1960s, painting began to use images again but treated them in a different way. By this time, mass media was a part of American life and the painters of the time, like Andy Warhol and Marisol, were creating artwork with images pulled right from advertisements or even other artists.

Eventually artists began to embrace using the camera in innovative ways that allowed for paintings that never would have been possible before. In the 1970s, photo-realism became the name of the game, and artists were celebrated for mimicking photographs all the way down to the tiniest details. Chuck Close, for example, creates incredibly detailed portraits of people, acne and all, which changed how people view portraits. He has even said of his art, "I am prepixel. They got it from me." So, after over a hundred years of worrying that the camera would replace painting, we now have painters who couldn't create the works of art they do without the camera!

OTHER INNOVATIVE DIGITAL TOOLS

There has never been a time in the world's history when technology was changing at such a rapid rate. Think about how movies have been viewed. For nearly eighty years, if you wanted to see a new movie you had to go to a movie theater. Then, in the 1980s, everyone had a VCR. DVD players slowly replaced VCRs in the 1990s. Now many computers do not even have slots for DVDs because they're becoming obsolete. Today, more people stream video through their computers or TVs, so we no longer need to own a physical copy of a movie. We now need a device that is capable of connecting to the internet. In this post-DVD world, there are more digital tools for innovation than ever before. Here are a few of the latest and greatest:

- **Google Cardboard.** One of the more exciting developments has been Google Cardboard. Whether you save money and simply fold your own or buy one of the numerous models out there, you can experience virtual reality with your smartphone. You can, for example, place your phone inside the cardboard and walk through the streets of Rome in virtual reality. The idea comes out of the spirit of open-source software (things developed for the common good), and Google is actively encouraging people to create more and new apps for virtual reality. Additionally, virtual reality is starting to come into the classroom. A great addition to your digital portfolio could be, for example, making a virtual reality Pompeii and then having documentation of how you took your entire class on a field trip to this ancient Roman city that was buried under a volcano thousands of years ago!
- **3-D Printing.** 3-D printers are more available now than they ever have been before. Many educators think that every student should have access to a 3-D printer because they offer so many innovations in the classroom. In *Forbes* magazine, contributor T.

J. McCue said, "Never mind the computer on every desktop, that's a given. In the near future, teachers and students will want or have a 3D printer on the desk to help them learn core Science, Technology, Engineering and Mathematics (STEM) principles." Printing in 3-D has applications beyond just being used for the sciences. It is being used in art classes, too.

The next generation of students will have countless new innovations to use when they are making school projects. Which of the innovations discussed interest you the most?

- **Massive Multiplayer Online Games (MMOs).** It may come as a surprise to you, but MMO games have been studied and it turns out many of the skills that are developed by playing these games are valued in the workplace. For example, open world games (games that allow the player to go anywhere) help develop patience and perseverance. Inherited from older games that required repetitive tasks, like *Tetris*, and then continued in games where you had to "level up" by accomplishing tasks like finding a certain number of coins, open world games have taken the concept to new extremes. If you can spend sixty hours doing the same activity in these games, creating a digital portfolio will be something you can easily accomplish. MMOs have also been linked to innovative thinking and strategic planning. Games like *Starcraft* take high levels of innovation.

  Sometimes, you may find yourself on the verge of losing in that moment of intense competition, and you create a new strategy just in time to defeat your opponent. Being able to make creative decisions and calculate the outcomes in real time is extremely valuable as a life skill. These games also, in contradiction of various stereotypes, increase leadership and socialization skills. In fact, today's multiplayer online games might even allow students who are a bit shy to open up and talk more with others, as there is a shared goal and experience to discuss. Also, coordinating a group of people toward a single goal is the ultimate in leadership.

Parents scolding you for spending too much time online playing games? Tell your parents that you are exercising dynamic problem solving!

Finally, gaming has been shown to help increase empathy (there is that word again). As games have evolved, game designers are starting to incorporate emotional elements like character development into their narrative stories. Getting emotionally invested in a character used to be strictly for what were considered "high art" forms like literature and film, but as games change and the machines that process them can accomplish more and more complex tasks, the world that the game takes place in becomes all the more full.

With the blink of an eye, technology changes. Today, there are digital portfolios, and tomorrow, who knows? To be ahead of other students, create a digital portfolio now. It could be the reason you get into the school or job of your dreams. Be sure to ask friends, family members, or teachers for their opinion. They want to see you succeed.

GLOSSARY

abstraction Dealing with ideas as opposed to things.

analog Not digital.

artifacts Things left over from an older time.

collaborative Being worked on together as a group.

cornerstone A stone at the corner of a building that usually has the date when the building was completed as well as a few objects inside of it.

curating Selecting carefully.

curriculum The courses studied in school.

disclaimer Writing that tells people what to expect, usually at the beginning of something; TV shows often have a disclaimer letting people know if there is violence or bad language.

document Any piece of paper that shows what you have done (like a test) or who you are (like a passport).

dynamic Something that is constantly being changed; the opposite of static.

empathy The ability to understand the feelings and situation of another person.

endorsement A recommendation or approval of something.

homogenization The act of making things the same.

inclusive Open to having more information; the opposite of exclusive.

interface Usually a screen that you interact with.

meticulously With great attention to detail.

nefarious Bad or evil.

nomenclature A system of naming things.

purview The range of things that can concern you; your teacher can be concerned about your grades, but how clean your room is would be outside of her purview.

rappel To go down the side of something, usually using a rope.

résumé A written record that people use to get a job, usually containing work, education, and other experience.

template A form that can be reused over and over.

testimonial A story about something that the speaker promises is true.

ubiquitous Very common; for example, McDonald's restaurants are ubiquitous throughout the world.

universal Applying to everyone or everything.

unkempt Messy.

unprecedented Describes something that has never happened before.

FOR MORE INFORMATION

American Institute of Graphic Arts (AIGA)
233 Broadway, 17th floor
New York, NY 10279
(212) 807-1900
Email: info@aiga.org
Website: http://www.aiga.org
The American Institute of Graphic Arts (AIGA) is an international
    professional association for design. AIGA has chapters all over
    the country and is passionate about education and empower-
    ing the next generation of designers.

British Columbia Technology for Learning Society
#206 - 6741 Cariboo Road
Burnaby, BC V3N 4A3
Canada
(604) 294-6886
Email: clientservices@reusetechbc.ca
Website: http://www.reusetechbc.ca
BC Tech for Learning Society offers refurbished computers to
    students and schools. It accepts donations and offers programs
    to help those in need.

Canadian Education Association
60 St. Clair Avenue East, Suite 703
Toronto, ON M4T 1N5
Canada
(866) 803-9549
Email: info@cea-ace.ca
Website: http://www.cea-ace.ca
The Canadian Education Association is an independent organiza-

tion that seeks to support innovation and leadership in education. Founded in 1891, the association wants to unlock the passion in each and every student.

College Board
250 Vesey Street
New York, NY 10281
(212) 713-8000
Email: info@collegeboard.org
Website: https://www.collegeboard.org
The College Board's goal is to help students receive higher education. The nonprofit is designed to advocate for both teachers and students.

d.school
Hasso Plattner Institute of Design
416 Escondido Mall
Building 550, Room 169
Stanford, CA 94305-3086
(650) 736-1025
Email: info@dschool.stanford.edu
Website: http://dschool.stanford.edu
Located at Stanford University, d.school is a place for people to meet and discuss innovation. The goal of the d.school is to bring together students from many different subjects and teach them ways to solve problems creatively.

George Lucas Educational Foundation
PO Box 3494
San Rafael, CA 94912
(650) 776-1005
Email: press@lucasedresearch.org
Website: https://www.edutopia.org

Edutopia is a group founded by George Lucas that wants to highlight innovation in education. Besides highlighting success stories, it also develops and evaluates methods for education.

WEBSITES

Because of the changing nature of internet links, Rosen Publishing has developed an online list of websites related to the subject of this book. This site is updated regularly. Please use this link to access the list:

http://www.rosenlinks.com/PROJL/solve

FOR FURTHER READING

Anderson, Denise. *Stand Out: Design a Personal Brand. Build a Killer Portfolio. Find a Great Design Job.* New York, NY: Pearson Education, 2016.

Blazek, Matthew J., Kat Kat Kadian-Baumeyer, Mario J. Llorente Leyva, Karimah Grayson, Dennis Yuzenas, Steve McCrea, Omar Vasile, Enrique Gonzalez, and Joshua Noel. *Quick Guide to Student Websites (4th Edition): A Letter to Directors of Sfchools about Digital Portfolios.* CreateSpace, 2016.

Cooper, Trudi. *Portfolio Assessment: A Guide for Students.* Praxis Education, 2014.

Daniels, Leonard, and Tamra Orr. *Web-Based Digital Presentations.* New York, NY: Rosen Publishing, 2016.

Fromm, Megan. *Digital Content Creation.* New York, NY: Rosen Publishing, 2015.

Fromm, Megan. *Gathering and Sharing Digital Information.* New York, NY: Rosen Publishing, 2015.

Greek, Joe. *Incredible Projects Using 3D Printing.* New York, NY: Rosen Publishing, 2015.

Hubbard, Rita. *Getting the Most out of MOOC: Massive Open Online Courses.* New York, NY: Rosen Publishing, 2015.

Kawa, Katie. *Mark Zuckerberg, Founder of Facebook.* New York, NY: Rosen Publishing, 2017.

McCrea, Steve. *The School Counselor's Guide to Digital Portfolios: Tools for Helping Students Make and Expand Free Websites.* CreateSpace, 2016.

Rauf, Don. *Virtual Reality.* New York, NY: Rosen Publishing, 2016.

Renwick, Matt. *Digital Student Portfolios: A Whole School Approach to Connected Learning and Continuous Assessment.* Kindle ed. Amazon, 2015.

BIBLIOGRAPHY

The Art Story. "Chuck Close." http://www.theartstory.org
/artist-close-chuck.htm.

Berger, Warren. "The Four Phases of Design Thinking." *Harvard Business Review*, July 29, 2010. https://hbr.org/2010/07/the
-four-phases-of-design-thin.

Byrne, Richard. "5 Good Options for Creating Digital Portfolios."
Free Technology for Teachers, March 5, 2014. http://www
.freetech4teachers.com/2014/03/5-good-options-for-creating
-digital.html#.WA9ewOErLVp.

Educators Technology. Educational Technology and Mobile Learning.
"A Beautiful Visual on the Impact of Technology on Today's
Classrooms." April 28, 2015. http://www.educatorstechnology
.com/2015/04/impact-of-technology-on-classrooms.html.

Facebook Business. "Increase Website Clicks or Conversions
Using Link Ads." https://www.facebook.com/business/a/online
-sales/page-post-link-ads.

Herold, Benjamin. "Technology in Education: An Overview."
Education Week, February 5, 2016. http://www.edweek.org
/ew/issues/technology-in-education.

Information Technology Services, Office of Teaching, Learning &
Technology. "Digital Tools Inspire New Classroom Innovation
and Collaboration." University of Iowa, February 2, 2016. https://
teach.its.uiowa.edu/news/digital-tools-inspire-new-classroom
-innovation-and-collaboration.

Jaschik, Scott. "Admissions Revolution." Inside Higher Ed,
September 29, 2015. https://www.insidehighered.com
/news/2015/09/29/80-colleges-and-universities-announce
-plan-new-application-and-new-approach.

Jokinen, Taru. "About ePortfolios—Practise, History and Different
Ways of Using Them." http://www.eife-l.org/activities/projects

/epicc/final_report/WP3/EPICC3_9_Portfolios%20in%20 Finland.pdf.

Lee, Joel. "5 Life Skills That Video Games Can Help You Develop." MakeUseOf, August 6, 2014. http://www.makeuseof .com/tag/5-life-skills-video-games-can-help-develop.

Naiman, Linda.. "Design Thinking as a Strategy for Innovation." Creativity at Work. http://www.creativityatwork.com/design -thinking-strategy-for-innovation.

Passuello, Luciano. "Brainwriting Is Brainstorming on Steroids." Litemind. https://litemind.com/brainwriting.

Passuello, Luciano. "Einstein's Secret to Amazing Problem Solving (and 10 Specific Ways You Can Use It)." Litemind. https:// litemind.com/problem-definition.

Santaguida, Vincent. "Folder and Naming Convention—10 Rules for Best Practice." eXadox, January 2010. http://www.exadox .com/en/articles/file-naming-convention-ten-rules-best-practice.

Vander Ark, Tom. "Every Student Should Have a Digital Portfolio." Getting Smart, June 26, 2015. http://gettingsmart .com/2015/06/every-student-should-have-a-digital-portfolio.

Virtue, Mark. "Zen and the Art of File and Folder Organization." How-To Geek, May 12, 2010. http://www.howtogeek.com /howto/15677/zen-and-the-art-of-file-and-folder-organization.

Washington and Lee University. "How to Create a Digital Portfolio." https://www.wlu.edu/career-development/students /professional-online-presence/digital-portfolios-and -professional-websites/how-to-create-a-digital-portfolio.

INDEX

ABOUT THE AUTHOR

IV Thurston is a marketing and public relations professional living in Buffalo, New York. Formerly a hiring manager for a design team, he is in a unique position to write about digital portfolios. Additionally, he has published widely in newspapers and journals and is also an accomplished poet.

PHOTO CREDITS